There....
And BACK Again

By Emily Grossman, MA

With love, all things are possible.

This book is dedicated to all of those who have given me love and all of those that I've loved....

Thank You!!!!!

I would like to thank my family, friends, and clinicians for always being behind me in my recovery.

To Sara Levenstein, my editor…I am so grateful for your help!

To my mom and dad - you are my light in my darkest hours.

To Pamela - your writing inspires mine, and I couldn't have a better sister.

To my Grandpa Morty - thank you for being so cute, and always listening to my stories.

To Aunt Susan, Uncle Steve, Dave and Melissa - you are the best family I could ever wish for.

To the rest of my relatives…ditto.

To my lifelong friends…I wish I could mention you all here…but you know that I love you all.

To Sherrie Schwab…for teaching me much of what is in this book and changing my life.

To Mrs. Collins- who helped me become the writer that I am.

To President Ikeda and my Buddhist practice thank you for changing my life.

And to all the many that I left out. . .
Thank you for making me who I am, and giving me the insight, hope, and courage to write this book, and change lives.

Introduction

You are a hero; a silent hero, yes, but a hero just the same. You are reading this book because you or someone you love has a mental illness and you want to help or be helped. This makes you a hero. You may not believe me. But it's true. You are a hero for identifying that you have a problem that needs help, and you are even more of a hero for seeking it out. One of the biggest problems that mental health professionals have in treating the illness is that there are tens of thousands of people who suffer without seeking out help at all. But, you are one of the brave ones, and that is to be commended.

Many people view their illness as a weakness or a character flaw. This is far from the truth. By reading this book, you are enlisting yourself in a fight against a very deadly disease. Weak people don't do things like that; that's the stuff that heroes are made of. Right now, each day, each moment, is difficult to get through. It is like running a marathon, and I want to be your coach. It would be my honor to join you on your journey back to wellness. For, although the disease is fatal if untreated, it is also extremely manageable with the proper care - much like diabetes.

Right now, you or someone you love is suffering a great deal. I am here to tell you that that suffering can be finite. There is a way out of the darkness. So let me throw you a flashlight so that you can see enough to find your way out. In this book, I will enlighten you as to the main ways that one can lift themselves from mental illness and go on to live a productive, happy life. So join me. I am not a psychiatrist; I am not a self-help guru. I am one of you - a regular person who has had my own struggles with mental illness, and has come out the other side. I believe that part of my mission here on earth is to help others who are struggling as I have. So, please, let me help you. I'll take your hand and we'll go through it one step at a time. We'll slowly begin to dig you out of your pain, and get you back on track again for a beautiful life. I know what it's like because I've been there. *I've been there and back again*.

Table of Contents

My Story

Sometimes, the best advice comes from those who have lived through something difficult. I have. And I've gotten back up afterwards. This is what qualifies me to advise you on how to deal with a mental illness. I'll go over the beginning of my experience with Bipolar disorder in this book. I am doing this in the hope that what you can take from my story is that *no matter how low you get, you, and only you, have the strength to rebuild your life into a beautiful story of triumph, love, and inner peace and joy.*

My story begins back in the fall of 1996. I was a freshman at the time at Emory University in Atlanta, Georgia. I had worked my butt off to get there. Things were going perfectly. I had a 4.0. I had just been selected as the only freshman to be a part of the advisory committee for student activities. I was in excellent shape. I had a wonderful new circle of friends. In short, everything was finally falling into place. I tell you this stuff not to brag, but simply to show you that mental health problems can happen to anyone, at any time in life, anywhere. It doesn't take a major tragedy or the death of a loved one to bring about this crisis. It is the nature of the beast that the chemicals get out of whack when they want to. This is why I want to emphasize that you cannot blame yourself for this illness. It is not your fault. My story is a testament to that.

I was putting a lot of pressure on myself. Pressure to be an A plus student. Pressure to look really good everyday. Pressure to keep up socially with a fast crowd. I had done this all of my life, and I didn't see any reason to stop. Anyway, it was my birthday, so I decided to go out with some friends. I had spent the couple of weeks before that partying and binge drinking. Don't get me wrong, I am definitely not an alcoholic by any stretch of the imagination. I was simply doing what many college freshman do - having fun (that sounds like the classic case of alcoholic denial, but after many years of therapy, I really think that if I were an alcoholic, it would have come out somewhere). So, I took about 10 of my friends out to a restaurant, where we got really drunk. Afterwards, we came home and I fell asleep. I slept, and slept and slept. The next morning, I could not wake up. So, I slept in, which would be fine, except the morning after that I could not wake up either. It got to the point where I was so afraid to get out of bed that I simply couldn't do it. I know that this concept may be hard to understand if you are reading this book and you have never had a mental illness. But, if you have, you probably understand this phenomenon quite well - much better than I understood it at the time. It scared me out of my mind. I was so scared that I had panic attacks in my bed. I called my mother, but I was so overwhelmed, that she couldn't calm me down.

I'll never forget the feeling; it was total helplessness. Anyone who's been through a panic attack knows - it is very scary. I literally thought that I was going to die. I couldn't go to class, and before this, I went to class everyday. My self-care fell away. I made appointments to see a therapist, but, I was really so panicked that all I did was cry. I just felt like I was being pulled slowly into a black hole, with no way out.

My mother came down to school to see if she could coach me back into health. She tried very hard, but what she would find is that this was bigger than what the two of us could handle. I attempted to commit suicide with pills, but before I could swallow them, I spit them out. I knew that I did not want my life story to end this way. This is when my mother decided to take me home for treatment. I flew home, and I remember my mother handing me sedatives to calm me down. I felt like a total failure. I felt as though I had ruined my life and everything that I had worked so hard for during my first 18 years.

I began being treated by a therapist and a psychiatrist, but to no avail. I had to be hospitalized twice in the period of two months. The hospitalizations were long; in fact one lasted nearly two weeks. It took me a very long time to get up. But, eventually, I did. With the care of therapists and psychiatrists, I went on medication and began working on some issues. I returned to school the next fall, and had some success. This began a lifetime struggle with bipolar disorder.

Since that time, a lot about me has changed. I did get my bachelor's and master's degrees. I became a teacher for a number of years, and then decided to transition into the mental health field as a recovery specialist. But, wherever I've been, I've had to battle through bouts of depression, anxiety, and hypo-mania. The real thing that changed for me was not finding a "magic pill" to cure me, but instead, learning how to manage my emotions. I hope that, just as I've helped many of my clients to do the same, I can help you with this book. If you work at it as I have, health and happiness can be yours, too.

Why Me?

So, you have been diagnosed with a mental illness. You are probably thinking, "How could this have happened to me?" There is no simple answer to this question. Everyone has some challenge in their lives - cancer, diabetes, divorce, death. It often seems like there is no rhyme or reason to how God metes out these fates, but that is one of the mysteries of this world that I do not have an answer for right now. This is your challenge. And, like any hurdle that you are faced with overcoming, the way you approach this obstacle can greatly impact your well-being and quality of life.

You are now faced with a challenge. You can accept it, and do everything in your power to live a healthy, productive life, or you can fight reality, try to "be normal," and set yourself up for a life of pain. I am hoping that this book will help prevent you from doing the latter, but the choice is truly yours.

So, am I just plain nuts?

You are not nuts. You are also not crazy, someone with a few screws loose, or any other euphemism that the mental illness-phobic masses will try to dub you. You have a chemical imbalance. And you are in good company. Many of the most creative geniuses in the entire human race have suffered with similar maladies.

What is a chemical imbalance? Put quite simply, it means that some of the chemicals in your brain are not functioning properly. You see, when you are scared, nervous, being chased by a lion, etc., your brain fires off a chemical called serotonin. This chemical puts your body into fight or flight mode, making it feel overly energized, ready to run, anxious, etc. This happens for a short time. Then, when the massive tiger bores of you, decides not to eat you, and goes away, most people's chemical just readjust, and everything is fine. If you have a mental illness, most likely, this does not happen in your brain. The chemicals do not dissipate, and you stay in that hyper-alert phase for a great deal of time. After an extended period of this, you come crashing down into a depression. This is not the paradigm for all types of mental illnesses, but it is certainly how depression, anxiety, and bipolar disorder work.

So there you have it. You are not weak, evil, lost, or out of touch. You have nothing to be ashamed of, and you did not do this to yourself. It was all a matter of faulty chemistry. So stop condemning yourself. There is no need to isolate. You are not a leper - you do not need to be quarantined.

And, luckily, due to the miracles of modern science, you can still live a productive life with meaningful relationships and activities. You just have to be dedicated to your health and decide that health is what you really want. It's a choice, and only you have the power to make it.

Acceptance

The first step to regaining your mental health is to accept. By this, I mean the wholehearted acknowledgment that you have a proclivity towards mind or mood disorders, and the commitment that you are willing to do whatever it takes to get well and stay well.

People spend their lives trying to run from their illness and, in turn, themselves. As a result, they never get the help that they need, and spend much of life in pain - madly dashing from one crisis to the next. How sad for these people that if they only accepted their situation, they could help themselves, and, in turn, put their lives back together.

I understand the urge to run. I also understand the urge to want to be "normal." But really, you are not as abnormal as you think. Many people have a mental illness; some just hide it well. In truth, there is no normal, there is no average; everyone is unique with their own attributes and qualities - positive and negative.

Acceptance is key; acceptance, and a willingness to get the help that you need. It takes time. There is no cure-all pill, no magic healer that can unleash the powers of the gods in order to cure you. But, once you have accepted that you have a problem which needs help, you are on the way to regulating the problem.

I say regulate because this is exactly what must be done. There is no known cure for mental illness. It must be controlled much as one would control their weight. Eating too many sweets can result in weight gain. Not following the advice that I've carefully outlined in this book can result in a loss of mental control, and the recurrence of the illness.

So, I hope that you are convinced that the best way through this crisis is to accept it. Acceptance is the key to getting you to the other side, and helping you to build a life worth living. Once you have committed to your health, you are ready to take the steps necessary to rebuild your life, and even make it more prosperous and happy than it was before. Just be patient; it will happen - you'll see.

Baby Steps

"A journey of a thousand miles begins with just a single step."~ Confucius

So, right now, you are probably not feeling at your best; otherwise, you wouldn't have picked up this book to begin with. I have news: it's okay. A mental illness is really a true, bona fide medical condition. And, just like if you had diabetes, heart disease, or any other major illness, you deserve, and are going to need, time to heal.

I know that it is difficult to grasp this concept because one cannot see a mental illness, and there are few tests to prove its existence. However, I promise, it is real. Mental illnesses are truly chemical imbalances in the brain. This is a fancy way of saying that some of the chemicals that insure proper brain functioning are a little out of whack. Is it permanent? Not necessarily. Can you heal from it? Yes. However, it will take a lot of patience on your part. You are going to have to take it in baby steps, not expecting your recovery to happen all in one day, but instead over time. Recovery is often a "two steps forward, one step backward" proposition. I like to think of recovery as kind of like the stock market when things are going right.

When the trend is upward, it still tends to go up and down,

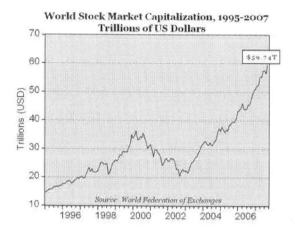

World Stock Market Capitalization, 1995-2007
Trillions of US Dollars

Source: World Federation of Exchanges

like this:

You can see that the trend between 1995 and 2007 is mostly up. However, that doesn't mean that we didn't have a couple of bad years in there where we had to sweat it out. That's just like recovery. You will get better, even if some days you take a few steps backward. The trend is "up."

In the rest of this book, I am going to outline things that you can do to help this upward trend move along at a better clip. However, again, be patient. You will get better in slow, baby steps; "one day at a time," not all at once.

Finding Your Anchor: Selecting the Right Health Care Professionals

OK, you might be thinking, what's the first baby step that I can take? Well, like any other illness, you are going to need to find health care professionals that you trust to treat it. However, here's where it is different: there is no "one" health care professional that can handle all of your concerns. It's going to take a team.

This team can consist of many people; however, the most common are: 1) a psychiatrist or nurse practitioner to prescribe medications and 2) a therapist. You may not want to stop there, though. Other professionals are helpful, including case managers, peer specialists, massage therapists, acupuncture therapists, art therapists, and the list goes on. So, how do you know who to employ to help you? The choice is yours. Whatever you think will help you probably will, so trust your instincts. However, the most important things for coping are having someone to talk to regularly, and having someone to prescribe medications.

A word about meds: many of you may not really want to take medication. I know that when I first was diagnosed, I sure didn't. I remember telling my mother that some of the greatest people in the history of the world had mental illness, and they didn't take meds. However, I believe now, after taking medications, that those people would have led much happier, more productive lives if they did take them. Medication doesn't kill your creative genius or anything like that. It just helps the chemistry to go back to normal so that you can function at a higher level. It still is your choice, and in some situations, your doctor may not recommend them, but if he or she does, I can only tell you that despite my doubts, medications have been a lifesaver for me.

Taking Control

There is a series of steps that you need to take to put your life together with two feet on the ground. The first is to make your own personal environment more conducive to your mental health. The most important way to do this is by structuring your life so that your health does not take the back burner to other things. Remember, mental health should be the most important goal, because it is the cornerstone on which all other aspects of your health rely.

Structure

In order to take control, you are going to have to live a fairly structured life. What do I mean by structure? Well, when we are in control of our mental health, they say we are "regulated." Regulated comes from the root word regular, and this is literally how the mental health client thrives - by being on a regular schedule. It is very important to do things at a regular time so as to not shock the body. This means eat, sleep, breathe, and take your medication at a regular time each day.

Many people who have a breakdown report that it began with several days of insomnia, the inability to eat, etc. Bipolar patients often work around the clock without sleep for days before they "crash." In these cases, the body is not regulated, and eventually, it shuts down. The body needs to be trained to function correctly, and when we upset our natural rhythm by changing our sleeping or eating patterns, we suffer the consequences.

In the case of a patient with mental health issues, this is especially true. Our chemistry and bodies are extremely sensitive. Thus, even minute changes in schedule can greatly affect our quality of life.

In my own personal experience, college was a difficult time. There was no set schedule. Classes were sporadic and often did not begin until late in the morning or in the afternoon. I would spend many nights out until the very wee hours of the morning. I would eat late at night and then go to bed, oftentimes not waking up until 12 p.m. for class.

My body did not appreciate this. It was very hard to regulate my medicine when I had no regular sleeping pattern. I was often foggy and moody, and I did not understand why. I then met a doctor that recommended that I be more stringent with my schedule. She said that I should go to bed at 12 a.m. and wake at 8 a.m. every day, without wavering too much from this policy. However, I was desperate to be a normal college student and fit in despite my mental illness. So, I tested these boundaries, and I paid the price with inconsistent attendance at class, mood swings, and erratic grades.

It was not until my senior year that I decided to take my health more seriously. I was desperate to graduate, so I went to my doctor for advice. She again emphasized the importance of a schedule. I took her advice. I ate at roughly the same time every day. I slept at the same time every night. I woke up and ran at 8 a.m. every morning. If I wanted to go out, I would make sure to be in by 1 a.m. And, fairly rapidly, my health improved.

On the contrary, after graduation, I became lax with my schedule. I did not wake up on time. I went to bed later and later. As a result, my health suffered. I lost the structure of classes. My life began to fall apart. Everyone told me to get a job, any job, just to stay regular, but I did not. I was too proud. I did not want to be a college graduate working at

Friendly's. So, I slipped back into depression. Now, I have a job. I have a regular schedule. I get up by 8 a.m. most days, exercise, and go to work. I am doing much, much better.

I do not suggest that you experiment with your mental health as much as I did. I hope that you can learn from my silly mistakes. Just because you need a structured lifestyle does not mean that you are not "normal." In fact, most of the high achievers of this world have some kind of regimen that they stick to daily. Professional athletes do it. So does the President of the United States. And in order to maintain your mental health, so must you. Think of it as basic training camp.

You may be saying to yourself that at this point, you are at an all-time low. You don't have a job, you are not in school, and you can barely get out of bed in the morning. I know what this is like. The only way out of that kind of depressive funk is to create your own schedule. During my senior year in college, my schedule was rather loose, with lots of down time. So, I devised the following strategy with my therapist, which I will pass onto you. It is a really powerful tool in rebuilding a productive life.

Here's how it works: each day should be structured around the things that are a necessity to maintaining health: eating, sleeping, and exercise. First, set a regular time that you are going to go to bed at night, and a regular time that you are going to get up in the morning:

8 a.m.: wake up

12 a.m.: bed

Next fill in the times for meals and exercise:

8 a.m.: wake up

run/ lift weights

9 a.m.: breakfast

9:30 a.m.: shower

12 p.m.: lunch

7 p.m.: dinner

12 a.m.: bed

Now, here's the key to having a productive day. Each day should be filled with two competency tasks and two self-soothing tasks. Competencies are things such as doing laundry, going food shopping, paying bills, etc. Notice you do not have to get everything done, just a couple of things every day to maintain positive, forward motion. Self-soothings include, but are not limited to: yoga, deep breathing, writing, bubble baths, video games, walks through the park, getting a manicure or pedicure, shopping, playing sports, playing cards, etc. I will give a list of possible soothing exercises in more detail later. The point is that one must do things to make himself or herself feel good.

Now, your schedule looks like this:

8 a.m.: wake up

8:10 a.m.: run/weight lift

9:00 a.m.: breakfast

9:30 a.m.: shower

10:30 a.m.: food shop and pick up medicines

12 p.m.: lunch

12:30 p.m.: write in my journal, or write a story

2:30 p.m.: do laundry

3:30 p.m.: get manicure

5:30 p.m.: return friends' phone calls

6:30 p.m.: dinner

7:30 p.m.: read

9 p.m.: watch TV

10 p.m.: look through the paper for a job

12 p.m.: bed

By structuring your time in this way, you are guaranteed to start to pick up the pieces and get your life back on track, having it move in a very productive, forward direction. Structure also prevents one from having too much time to worry, something that people with depression seem to be very good at doing. Once life becomes more structured and regimented, you are on your way to regaining your mental health and sense of purpose in life. At this point, it is time to take control of other aspects of your health so that you can continue on the path to wellness.

The "Meat and Potatoes" of Recovery

As a recovery specialist, it is my job to see that my clients are using techniques or coping skills in order to handle their difficult emotions. If they do not, they are more prone to cope with their mental illnesses in unhealthy ways, such as smoking or doing drugs, overeating, gambling, etc.

In my own recovery process, I searched long and hard for some way to cope. Finally, I discovered DBT, or dialectical behavioral therapy, which is really fancy psychologist speak for coping skills.

The most important thing that your therapist is going to teach you is that you must change your way of thinking in order to create a life worth living. If you are chronically depressed, for example, you are probably involved in a vicious cycle of negative beliefs.

The key to moving on with your life in a healthy way is to change those thoughts and beliefs so that you feel more hope, more joy, and more self-confidence. Depressed people generally distort things. They basically believe that they've always felt the way they do now, and that it is never going to change. They will never be productive members of society, they will never have happy lives, and they never have. You really have to cut these beliefs off right at the roots, and weed them out one by one. This type of thinking will keep you stuck forever.

So, how do you start? Well, cognitive behavioral therapy will certainly help, and I will go over that with you shortly. However, on a more basic level, I can tell you what happened to me and how I changed my own beliefs. I came to a point that, after seven years of struggling with a mental illness and believing that my life was going nowhere, I finally hit rock bottom. I had no job, I was living in a very undesirable living situation, and I had no self-esteem. So, I finally made the decision once and for all that this was not going to be the way that I spent the rest of my life. I was no longer going to be the victim of my mental health issues. I was never going to get that low again. I was going to get the better of the issues, rather than allowing them to get the better of me.

I took a part-time job at a law firm just to give myself structure while I was looking for a full-time job.

Although my doctors were uncertain as to whether I was going to be able to handle a full-time job, I decided that failure was not an option for me. I knew that I would accept no less than being able to support myself. I had a college degree, and there was no reason why I should be unable to get a full-time job. It would mean tolerating the pain of a new experience and getting up early to go to work. However, I knew it was the only way for me.

In short, in the words of my therapist, I made a choice. I made a choice to function and live a productive life. I made a choice to take the steps to build a life worth living. I knew that I wanted a life full of meaningful relationships and activities, and I would not settle for anything less. I would not accept failure.

Once I had made the choice to stop being a victim, things improved in my life. I did find that full-time job and I forced myself to get there on time and do a wonderful job while I was there. Slowly, my self-confidence began to increase. I realized that I had something to offer others, so I began to develop new friendships. I found new places to go with these friends. I began dating again, because I had more self-esteem. I was able to move from my living situation to a house on the beach with two other girls my age, because I had a way to support myself. My relationship with my family completely changed as well. They could relate to me as an equal, not someone that they had to worry about and take care of. In short, my life totally transformed because I changed my thinking. I made a choice, and that one choice has changed me from an underachiever to someone who doggedly pursues her goals and wants the most out of life. It is not always easy to do this. There are still times when I would probably rather stay in bed. However, I do not like the person that stays in bed and doesn't take care of herself. And, I need to like myself. So, I push through those beginning-of-the-morning blues, head to the gym, and live a very fulfilling, wonderful existence while making a difference in children's lives.

You can do it, too. I am not a superhero; I am just an average person with a chemical imbalance who decided to make a choice to live the life that I was intended to live. I decided to stop accepting the impulse to give in and not function. I decided to stop using my illness as an excuse. But mostly, I decided that I deserved no less than to live the beautiful life that I had right in front of me. I decided that wishing things were different was getting me nowhere, and the only way out of my sad, depressed existence was to change my thinking and start living again. It took some time, but not nearly as much as I thought, and it took some effort, but again, not nearly as much as I thought, and I was able to learn to take care of myself and live the high-functioning life that I'd always dreamed of living. And I decided to NEVER GO BACK. It's a choice. Now it's your turn to make it.

Cognitive Behavioral Therapy

As I have explained earlier, the basic approach behind cognitive behavioral therapy is the following: when you change the way you think, your mood, and ultimately your behaviors, will follow. As Shakespeare explains in Hamlet, "for there is nothing either good or bad but thinking makes it so" ("Hamlet", Act 2, Scene 2). The way we interpret events creates our feelings, which then creates our mood. When we feel depressed, it is because our negative way of interpreting events brings us to this place. As Dr. David D. Burns discusses in his book, *Feeling Good*:

> ...the negative thoughts that flood your mind are the actual cause of your self-defeating emotions. These thoughts are what keep you lethargic and make you feel inadequate. Your

negative thoughts, or cognitions, are the most

frequently overlooked symptoms of your

depression. These cognitions contain the key

to relief… (Burns, 29).

Let us take the example that you are being transferred

in your job. You were working for one branch of the

company, and your boss comes to you and says that you are

now going to be transferred to another branch. You don't

like your boss, and you have often hinted that you would

appreciate the transfer. There are two ways to look at this

situation. The way that you look at it will certainly affect

your mood.

You could, on the one hand say, "I am so fortunate

because today, I am being moved to a different branch of the

company. Here is a chance to prove myself to a new boss

who I may like, and even get ahead in the company. I will be leaving my old boss, who I have trouble getting along with, and I will be able to turn over a new leaf. You then turn your mind to doing the best job possible in your new position, and you feel good.

However, there is another way to interpret this situation. You can start to feel fear: "I don't adjust well to new situations; thus, I am going to hate this job," or "What if I do not like anyone that I work with at the new job?" Then, you begin to doubt yourself: "Does my boss here hate me so much that he requested that I get transferred?" Suddenly you begin to classify yourself as inadequate - you are not a good worker at your old job, and you will not be good at this new job either. You begin to be overwhelmed by negative emotions, and suddenly you become despondent and depressed.

If you are depressed, chances are you respond to situations more like the second interpretation rather than the first. This leads to lowered feelings, and a less-than-chipper mood. The only way out is to begin to change your thoughts so that you can change your feelings. As I have said before, there are several books that deal extensively with this topic. One that has helped me very much is a book called *Mental Health Through Will Training*, by Dr. Abraham A. Low, MD. Another is *Feeling Good*, by Dr. Burns.

The best way out of your lowered feelings is to learn to catch yourself in the negative thought patterns and change them. Dr. Low's approach is to have his patients memorize a set of sayings that you can say to yourself when you catch yourself falling into a negative thought pattern. He suggests a format in which you begin by describing the event in full detail, ending with "That's where I began to work myself up." Next, you describe any feelings and sensations that you had as a result of getting worked up. For example, you may have noticed stiffness in your neck or tightness in your chest. After that, you explain what you said to yourself to calm down. In Dr. Low's book, there are literally hundreds of sayings, know as "spottings," that you learn as you attend the meetings of his group, "Recovery Incorporated."

In another book, *Skills Training for Treating Borderline Personality Disorder*, by Marsha Linehan, the author suggests that patients follow an outline in which you first describe the emotion that you are feeling and then rate it on a scale of one to one hundred. Next, you explain the prompting event for the emotion (who, what, when and where). Then, you explain the interpretations that you have made about the situation. After this, you explain your body changes and sensing, and your body language. Next, you explain your action urges, or what you want to do or say. Finally, you say what you said or did in the situation, and explain the after-affect that this had on you. This is another good way to track the way that your thoughts or interpretations about certain events affect your moods. Dr. Low's approach is perhaps more thorough in that it gives you canned phrases that you can say back to yourself when you begin the vicious cycle of negative thoughts.

As my therapist, Sherry Schwab, would explain, the main goal of cognitive behavioral therapy is to stop "negatively jump-starting yourself" through negative thoughts. She often compares our thoughts to a kaleidoscope. When you move the wheel of the kaleidoscope, you often see things in a different way. The purpose of cognitive behavioral therapy is to get you to move the wheel and change your perspective so that you are not continually seeing things in such a bad light, which creates

bad moods.

Whichever method you choose to start changing your

perspective, you are going to need support to do so. This is

why I have found that in addition to a therapist and

medication, support groups are often extremely helpful.

Support Groups

One of the most heartbreaking things about mental

illness is the way it makes people isolate themselves. They

feel as though they are inferior, so they avoid contact with

other people. It is often comforting to know that you are not

alone, and that there are other people that share your

problem. Support groups are often a safe way to get back

into the world, and begin to trust that you can be social again.

I have been a member of two support groups in my life, both of which I found extremely helpful. The first was called DBT. The other was Recovery Incorporated.

Before I discuss each of these groups, there are a few caveats that I must make when it comes to the support group. The first is to make sure that it is a support group, not a "bitching session." Let's face it: depressed people are often, well, depressed. As a result, the tendency is to try to find a place to vent. This type of group is not truly helpful; it is unproductive and non-therapeutic as much as the typical "venting therapy" is unproductive.

The type of group that you want should probably be cognitive behavioral in its approach. More importantly, it should be a solution-oriented group. What do I mean by this? Well, it should be a group in which problems are discussed, but solutions are sought. Venting should be kept to a minimum so that problems can be resolved. No group takes the place of the clinician. It is an adjunct to the therapist and psychiatrist. The group's purpose is to give one a sense of belonging in an illness that normally leaves people feeling quite alone.

One of the groups that I have mentioned, Recovery Incorporated, was truly a godsend for me. I discovered it when I was in my second to last semester of college, when I needed it the most. The group was founded by Dr. Abraham Low, an ingenious psychiatrist, who saw that his patients were not getting better after repeated hospitalizations. He wanted to create a way that these patients could stay out of the hospital and live productive lives. So, he formed a support group, which he prescribed along with his regular therapy sessions. Dr. Low's method predates cognitive behavioral therapy, but that, in essence, is what he preaches.

The group meets weekly, and each member discusses one problem that they had during the week. It is a very strict format in which the speaker is timed, and must present in the following order:

A) Explain the events that happened, ending with "That was when I began to work myself up"

B) Describe the physical sensations that you had

C) Explain what "spottings" you did

D) State what you would have done before recovery training

A spotting is a saying that one repeats in order to calm down. The spottings are discussed at meetings, and can be found in Dr. Low's books, the most important of which is called *Mental Illness Through Will Training.* Some examples of spottings are: "Bear the discomfort and the comfort will come," or "Perfection is a hope, a dream, and an illusion." Each member gives their "example" before a panel, and the members all then take turns spotting on the example. The spottings tell the person who gave the example ways to calm down in a difficult situation. One of the most important things that the group stresses is the importance of endorsing oneself for using recovery training, or just doing productive things in general. If someone does not endorse themselves, it is considered sabotage.

I found this group extremely helpful because it really helped me learn how to calm myself down when I was feeling overwhelmed by my emotions. I was one who often looked to others for help when my illness was getting the best of me, and this group gave me phrases that I could say to myself in order to feel better. I began handling myself better, I felt better, lost weight, and graduated college, all because I had new confidence in the fact that I could help myself out of difficult moments.

The other group that I was a member of was DBT, or dialectical behavioral therapy. In this group, we worked from a workbook written by Marsha Linehan, Ph.D., who was also a former mental health client. The general goal for this therapy is to "learn and refine skills in changing behavioral, emotional, and thinking patterns associated with problems in living; that is, those causing misery and distress." This was stated more succinctly by my own therapist, who said: "Your goal is to create a life worth living with meaningful relationships and activities." The behaviors that this therapy seeks to decrease are interpersonal chaos, labile emotions and moods, confusion about the self, cognitive dysregulation, and impulsiveness. The therapy seeks to change this by providing the client with the skills necessary to live in a less chaotic, less impulsive, less emotional way.

The best thing about this therapy is that it is structured, and as I have told you several times, the "mental health client" thrives on structure. The therapy is set up in four modules. Each patient gets a binder, which gives information on each module. The modules are: mindfulness, distress tolerance, interpersonal effectiveness, and emotional regulation.

Mindfulness skills are at the heart of the program. The first couple of pages teach the client how to get control of his or her mind using mindfulness skills. Mindfulness is really learning to stay in the moment and not let your emotions flood you out. It is learning to observe, describe, and participate fully in each moment without going too far in the future, or too far in the past. It is also learning to be nonjudgmental of yourself and others, be mindful in the way you do things with your attention fully in them, and interact in an effective way with the environment around you. Once one masters mindfulness, which takes quite a great deal of mental attention and focus, one can learn to observe his or her emotions without getting attached to them and let them wash through like waves in the sea.

The next concept that the client learns is **distress tolerance**. To the impulsive or suicidal person, this section is a godsend. It teaches you how to get through a crisis through distraction techniques such as activities, contributing, comparisons, "opposite of the emotion," pushing away thoughts, and sensations, until you are able to accept the crisis and move through it. It also teaches skills to use in order to improve the moment. One can learn to improve the moment by using imagery, finding meaning in the situation, through prayer, relaxation, one thing at a time, taking a vacation, or encouragement. All of these things are described in more detail as the patient continues treatment, but for our purposes here, I will just provide you with the bare-bones explanation. The details can be learned in Marsha Linehan's *Skills Training Manual for Treating Borderline Personality Disorder*.

The next part of distress tolerance involves learning to become willing rather than willful. Willingness, according to Ms. Linehan, means "doing just what is needed in each situation in an unpretentious way. It is focusing on effectiveness." After this, the client learns about the basic principles of accepting reality with, my favorite segment, an introduction to radical acceptance. Radical acceptance means deciding to tolerate the moment, acknowledging what is, and letting go of fighting reality. It involves making a choice to accept what is instead of rejecting reality. It involves an inner commitment to accept something, no matter how difficult that may be.

After this, the client learns **emotional regulation skills**. My therapist calls this the "meat and potatoes" of DBT. The client receives a lot of homework during this segment of the therapy. The homework is to observe and describe emotions using a format that is not unlike Dr. Low's. The sheet for the client to fill out looks like this:

Prompting Event for My Emotion

Interpretations

Body Changes and Sensing

Body Language

Action Urges

What I said or did in the situation

What after-effect does the emotion have on me

The general goal of this part of DBT is to help you identify your thoughts and emotions, and learn how they impact you, so that you can stop being the victim of them. This is a critical part of the therapy. So many of us walk around on a hairline trigger; we feel something, and then we react. This is the cause of so much suffering. Learning to accept our emotions as temporary and fleeting prevents us from getting too attached to them, and helps us to stop reacting in such a negative way.

The final section of DBT is the section on **Interpersonal Effectiveness**. We all need a lesson in this whether we are depressed or not depressed. It helps you to learn how to deal with interpersonal situations in such a way that you maintain your self-respect. It involves acting in a way that makes you feel moral, capable, and effective. It also examines factors that reduce our interpersonal effectiveness, and how to get through them so that you can get what you want. Sounds like DBT is a class that everyone should really take, huh? Why don't they make it mandatory in all high school health classes or something? Truly, a comprehensive self-help seminar such as this one could benefit everyone.

If you do have access to the Internet, you can learn more about the group by going to www.dbtselfhelp.com, or feel free to buy the following books: 1) *Skills Manual for Treating Borderline Personality Disorder* by Marsha M. Linehan, Ph.D. (DBT is really for everyone, but was originally designed for those with BPD) or 2) *The Dialectical Behavior Therapy Skills Workbook* by Matthew McKay, Ph.D., Jeffrey C. Wood, Psy.D, and Jeffrey Brantley, MD.

These resources will tell you all that you need to know about how to cope with difficult emotions better.

Relaxation Strategies

So, let's say you need something immediately to calm you down. You are in too much of a crisis to go online or wait for the books that you ordered to help you cope. Well, here are some tried-and-true relaxation strategies that I've used successfully myself and with my clients.

1. Square Breathing

The first technique that I am going to teach you today is known as square breathing. With this technique, you will find relaxation because it brings you back to the present moment. Every time that we worry, what we are really allowing ourselves to do is let our minds carry our thoughts too far into the past, or too far in the future. Here's a technique to keep your mind in the here-and-now, so that you are not worrying too much and ruminating about things that you cannot change.

Here's how to do the exercise:

Visualize a square in your mind, like this one:

As you are picturing one side of the square, breathe in for a count of four. Next, hold for four. Then let your breath out for a count of four. Finally, hold for four. Repeat at least ten times. Do this exercise anytime that you are feeling anxious, and noticing that your thoughts are not in the present moment.

2. Sight-Sound-Touch

This is another exercise for bringing yourself back into the present moment. Here's how you do it: look around the room. Every time you see something, say in your mind, "sight." Every time you feel something, say "touch." Every time you hear something, say "sound" in your mind.

This exercise works because, again, you are breaking into the ruminating thoughts, and bringing your mind back to the present moment. This is the only moment that matters. Remember that.

3. Radical Acceptance

Have you ever had a situation in your life go so wrong that you end up saying to yourself, "In the movie of my life, this is not the script that I ordered?" It happens to all of us. However, it is our job to tolerate difficult events without making them worse by letting our emotions get out of control. Marsha Linehan, Ph.D., often tells people that pain is a part of life, but suffering is pain plus non-acceptance of this pain. Pain is tolerable. It is suffering that is so difficult to tolerate.

So how do we experience the pain without the suffering? We can do this through a skill called radical acceptance. Radical acceptance is total and complete acceptance of a situation or event in the here-and-now. It does not mean that we are judging that event as good. It just means that we are accepting that things are exactly as they are meant to be in this moment.

As Marsha Linehan says, "Freedom from suffering requires acceptance from deep within of what is. Let go of fighting reality. Acceptance is the only way out of hell. Pain creates suffering only when you refuse to accept the pain. Deciding to tolerate the moment is acceptance." (Linehan, 176). She also explains that sometimes the way to radically accept something is to turn the mind to that over and over and over. As she explains: "Acceptance of reality as it is requires an act of CHOICE. It is like coming to a fork in the road. You have to turn your mind towards the acceptance road and away from the 'rejecting reality' road. You have to make an inner commitment to accept. The commitment to accept does not itself equal acceptance. It just turns you toward the path. But, it is the first step.

You have to turn your mind and commit to acceptance over and over and over again. Sometimes, you have to make the commitment many times in the space of a few minutes." (Linehan, 176). This is the way out of suffering, and the way towards emotional freedom.

Self-Soothing

More than the care of others, it is your own self-care that will get you well. Chances are, part of the reason why you got sick in the first place is because you were neglecting yourself in some way. I do not say this in an accusatory way; in our busy lives, it is often hard to remember to care for ourselves properly. However, this mental health crisis is the universe's way of saying, "It's time to slow down and learn to care for yourself properly." What do I mean by self-care? Of course, there are the basics: three meals, regular exercise, sleep, and medication. And again, I would like to make another plug for structure. But, one can live a very structured life with all of the basics in place, and still have no idea of how to care for him or herself. One must learn to incorporate self-soothing acts in one's life in order to get well. What is a self-soothing act? It is different for different people. It may be a yoga class, a bath, meditation, prayer, polishing one's nails, watching the big game, writing, playing sports, or many other things. Picture someone you love coming over and taking very good care of you for a day. Maybe it is your mom or your lover. What are they doing for you? Are they bathing you? Are they putting you in your silkiest pajamas? Are they making you chicken soup? Whatever they are doing for you, you must learn to do for yourself. Make a list of all of your favorite things to do, and start doing them. I know that right now, you probably have no desire to do anything, but wellness is in the "doing." You must begin to force yourself to do soothing things again, and slowly, you will find that you enjoy doing them.

This can be a growth time for you; one where you become more connected with yourself, and what you like to do to feel better. It is about being your own mom, your own lover, and treating yourself with the kind of tenderness that you would get from them. This self-soothing will do two things. First, it will make you feel better. Next, it will get you moving, and out of the slump of non-doing that your depression or other mental illness has created. Make a small list at first if you cannot think of many soothing things that you could do for yourself. The list will grow as you begin doing the things that you have already put down. Soon you will find the list will grow exponentially, and so will your sense of inner peace. Here is a list of some of the things that I have taken joy in doing, and some that I have not yet tried. Hopefully, it will help to get you started.

Pleasant Activities:

1. bath

2. collecting things

3. vacations

4. yoga

5. dating

6. movies

7. jogging

8. walking

9. music (playing or listening)

10. sunbathing

11. laughing

12. reading

13. being in nature

14. dancing

15. eating

16. practicing karate, judo

17. repairing things

18. gardening

19. swimming

20. doodling

21. exercise

22. going to a party

23. shopping

24. playing sports

25. flying kites

26. having family get-togethers

27. riding a motorcycle

28. sex

29. camping

30. singing

31. arranging flowers

32. practicing religion

33. going to the beach

34. going skating

35. going sailing

36. traveling

37. doing art

38. doing needlepoint

39. driving

40. going to clubs

41. going hunting

42. flirting

43. doing arts and crafts

44. making a gift for someone

45. watching a sport

46. writing

47. sewing

48. cooking

49. planning a party

50. hiking

51. going out to dinner

52. gardening

53. kissing

54. watching children play

55. playing with kids

56. going to plays and concerts

57. prayer and meditation

58. furniture building

59. watching TV

60. watching a movie

61. collecting shells

62. going to see a sport

63. teaching

64. photography

61. fishing

62. flying a plane

63. playing with animals

64. surfing the web

65. writing a letter/e-mail

66. acting

67. writing a diary

68. cleaning

69. going out with the girls/guys

70. getting dressed up

71. going into a sauna/ hot tub

72. going on a picnic

73. playing cards

74. doing crossword puzzles/ riddles

75. making a photo album/ scrapbook

76. talking on the phone

77. going to museums

78. lighting candles

79. saying "I love you"

80. getting a massage

81. going skiing/snowboarding

82. playing a video game

83. going bowling

84. doing woodwork

85. debating

86. going to lunch with a friend

87. going to a theme park

88. thinking about a crush

89. going horseback riding

Living in the Now

Now that you have decided that you would like to get on the path to wellness, it is important that you begin doing it, one day at a time. You are probably used to living a life of intense emotional pain, and it is time to change this. The best way that I know how to do this is by living in the now. What do I mean by this? Well, I am myself a novice, so I will teach you what I know of it, and hopefully we can learn together. When we are suffering emotionally, chances are, we are looking too far in the past and beating ourselves up, or looking too far into the future and predicting all future pain that we are going to experience. Both of these states of existence are not good, and detrimental to our mental health.

The only time that we should really focus on, for the good of our mental health, is now. Think about this: do you really have any problems now? Yes, you have things hanging over your head; however, right now, at this exact moment, is anything really wrong? Look around the room that you are in right now. Listen to the hum around you. Smell the air. Is anything really wrong at this exact second? The answer is probably no. In the now, nothing is wrong. There are no problems right now. Problems are a part of our future or past. If we exist in the now, there is nothing that we cannot conquer. Even if a problem were to come up and slap us in the face, chances are, by being in the now, we could handle it.

Think about driving, for instance. When you are focusing solely on the road, are you a good driver? Are you better at driving this way than when you are on your cell phone? What happens if you look too far behind you when you drive? Aren't you likely to miss what is in front of you and crash? Now what if you look too far ahead of you and don't focus on the road directly in front of you? You will most likely miss something and run into it. We work the same way in our lives. If we are too distracted, if we look too far ahead of ourselves or too far behind ourselves, we crash. It is only when we are focused on being in the present moment that we are really in the "driver's seat" of our own life and in a better position to "steer" ourselves in the right direction. Two phenomenal books on this subject are: *The Power of Now*, by Eckart Tolle, and *The Present*, by Spencer Johnson. I really recommend that you add these books to your required reading list and take their message to heart: the only time that matters is now.

Riding the Waves of Your Emotions: On Learning to Surf

In order to survive a mental illness, you really need to become a professional surfer. What do I mean by this? Well, you really need to learn how to ride the waves of your emotions. I always think of this saying that I learned in Recovery Incorporated: "Feelings will rise and fall and run their course as long as we do not attach danger." Think about the wisdom of this. When you are afraid of something and you keep on thinking about that thing over and over again, what happens? You get more afraid. You get more and more worked up. Your inner voice is screaming "danger," and the chemicals in your brain are actually responding by firing off to give you the adrenaline to get out of that situation. On the contrary, if, when you experience fear, worry, or anger, you should just accept it as a feeling. If you do not let it carry you away, you will not be derailed by it, you will not fall off of your metaphorical "surf board." Most importantly, by doing this, the feeling will pass much more quickly.

I know what you are thinking. This seems so much easier said than done. When you are angry, you are angry; when you are worried you are worried; and there is little that you, I, or anyone can do to change it. This is not really so. There are many techniques that you, the surfer, can use to stay on the board. The first is a technique that I referred to earlier, created by Dr. Low, called spotting. If, when you start to feel an intense emotion coming over you, you spot it, or catch yourself by saying, "Feelings will rise and fall and run their course as long as we don't attach any danger," you will almost be able to feel inside how quickly you can actually "work it down." A physical and biochemical shift actually takes place due to this thought. If spotting seems too difficult, try meditation or deep breathing. When you feel yourself getting overtaken by an emotion, find a quiet place, close your eyes and begin to breathe in and out, slowly counting your breaths as you go. If this is not possible, try a mindfulness exercise. Put your full attention in the now, focusing on exactly what you are doing. If you are driving, drive. If you are washing the dishes, wash the dishes. Repeat to yourself "Right now, I am driving." Look at the car ahead of you and actually say the license plate letters and numbers out loud. This should take your mind off of your emotion and re-center you so that the danger messages start to subside. Another technique is to say to yourself: "This is just an emotion." Experience the emotion without judging it. Accept that you have the emotion without thinking about or trying to change it. This, too, will help the emotion pass. Don't take it too seriously.

Regardless of which method you choose, the point is to become skillful at navigating through your emotions rather than getting sucked into them. My therapist always likes to say, "Are you riding the horse, or are you letting it ride you?" You can get on top of that bucking bronco of an emotion, take the reins and get it under control, or you can let it rattle you to the point that you get thrown. The choice is yours. In order to improve your mental health, and your life, the goal is to view your emotions as old friends. When they come, greet them at the door, introduce yourself, and say, "Hello anger, today you are not going to wreak havoc on my life." Once you are aware of your emotions, you can get control, and not be taken for a ride. They will pass much, much more quickly that way.

The Dangers of Anger and Temper

As I have stated earlier, when a person has a mental illness, they experience emotions a lot more intensely than others may experience them. This is why, in order to stay healthy, one must really try to keep intense emotions at bay. This takes effort, but one way to do it can be by eliminating the drama and avoiding major arguments with people. As Dr. Low would say, a patient with a mental health issue cannot afford "the luxury of temper." This means that while others can get into fights all the time, and not really be impacted, those of us with mental health issues will suffer with symptoms of our illness after a major fight.

Think about it: have you ever gotten into a disagreement with someone, and tried to prove that you were right, and later on you got a major headache? This headache was a "symptom." These symptoms can affect us for days after getting into a scuffle with someone. They can make us end up in bed rather than out of our house doing healthy, happy activities. The symptoms can lead to a depression and a relapse all because we were so intent on proving that we were right. Dr. Low calls this urge to prove that we were right a symbolic victory. Some people spend their whole lives on one big crusade to find symbolic victories. They live an empty, angry, symptom-filled life. Many times it is also a short life because the symptoms that come from this kind of lifestyle can greatly reduce one's lifespan.

To maintain your mental health, it is important to begin to choose peace over power. You must learn to live and let live. Drama and anger and temper must be curbed for the sake of your health. This may be harder for some than others. However, learning to avoid the temper-filled argument and learning to strive for peace in your life can be freeing. It takes a lot of energy to be angry. It takes a lot of energy to fight, to try to prove your point, or to strive to be right all the time. No one is right all of the time. So, let go of useless anger and fighting that doesn't work in your life. Choose your mental health. With this approach, you will be right all of the time, because you are striving for a larger goal than just to win an argument; you are working on your health and well-being. And mental health is something worth working towards.

Relationships

Since we are on the subject of relationships and getting what we want, I must touch upon this issue next. When one has any illness, it definitely puts a strain on those who care about you. They feel the need to take care of you and to help you. This is a vulnerable time in your life, and you certainly cannot get through mental illness alone. In fact, one of the key factors in recovery is having a good support system. This said, I must warn against a trap that many fall into: the need to be taken care of. You are the only one who can take control of your mental illness. Family and friends can have great intentions, but they cannot do it for you. They cannot fully take care of you; they will try, as they love you, and see you struggling. However, only you have the power to get well.

This said, I must go a step further. While recovering from a mental illness, you are not in the state to form a lasting, healthy, committed relationship. It really is difficult to accept this, because for many of us, when we feel needy and sick, we just want to connect with someone, and look to someone to make it all better for us. We want to be coddled, taken care of, and loved. THIS IS CODEPENDENCE. It is unhealthy, and will lead to pain. It will lead to all kinds of manipulative attempts to try to get the object of affection to take care of us. It will lead to a strain on the object of our affection. It will lead to an unhealthy relationship in which the person who is caring for us does it because he or she feels as though it is their job. Furthermore, there are certain types of people who are willing to care for us in our times of need. Our family will do it out of pure love. However, someone who is looking to be in a relationship with a needy, sick person comes to that relationship with motives of their own. They are insecure, they need to feel needed, and they need to have power over someone in order to feel good. There are books written about codependent, love-addicted relationships. One good one is called *Facing Love Addiction*, by Pia Mellody. However, the long and short of it is: stay out of a relationship until you are stronger.

If you are involved with someone already, they have a lot of learning to do along with you in order to figure out their role in your recovery. Again, they cannot heal you. Your recovery is your responsibility. However, they need to learn about the illness as well, so that they can figure out how to handle the delicate situations that will come up during your treatment. Reading this book may help with that. Please be as patient with those that love you as possible.

The Choice

As I have alluded to earlier, you have a very important choice to make. Mental illness can be a very debilitating, crippling disease. It can shatter one's life, and make one become incapacitated. Some people who have mental illness fall into a dark hole and never get out. Yet, others are highly successful entrepreneurs, actors, scientists, and doctors. What separates those who are successful in spite of mental illness from those who are not? Put simply, it is a choice.

My therapist introduced me to this concept, and it radically changed my life. She put the choice in front of me: do I want to live as a disabled person for the rest of my life or do I want to deal with the limitations of my illness, take my medications, and listen to my doctors so that I can lead a healthy and productive life? I chose the latter, and I hope you will do the same. However, I must be very clear that this is a commitment that you must make for the rest of your life. You must really decide that you don't want to spend the rest of your life in hospitals, in bed, overmedicated, and underachieving. You must choose to get out of bed every morning. You must choose to function, and make this your priority above all else. Once you have resolved that you are going to live a full life in spite of mental illness, you can surely do it. But, it involves a conscious decision to get well, and stay well.

This choice that I speak of is quite paradoxical. On the one hand, taking control of one's life involves taking responsibility for oneself. It involves discipline, vigilance, and a commitment to live life in an adult way. However, this very same choice is liberating. No longer must you rely on your family or a doctor's care. You make your own choices. And you are so in control that those around you feel comfortable allowing you to make your own choices. Trust me, I've lived both ways, and I have found nothing as empowering as taking control of my own life. It's better than Prozac, more calming than a tranquilizer, and more rewarding than sitting on the couch pouting and making others feel sorry for you.

If all of this is not enough motivation to make you want to get back in the driver's seat of your life, then maybe the next thing that I am going to share will be. It is a very powerful tool that my therapist taught me - the modified pro and con list. The list involves four columns: Pro Being Sick, Con Being Sick, Pro Not Being Sick, and Con Not Being Sick. This list involves helping you sort out some of the reasons why you might be staying sick, so that you can get yourself out of the rut. It looks something like this:

Pro Being Sick

- people will feel sorry for me and take care of me
- I will get attention
- I won't have to take care of my responsibilities
- I won't have to set goals

Con Being Sick

- people will look down on me for not "pulling my weight"
- I won't feel good about myself because I am not living up to my potential
- I won't attract other competent people

- I won't be trusted with my decisions

- I won't be able to make money, get the degree, or accomplish any of my other goals

- I won't live up to my potential

- I will be bored from sitting around all day and not accomplishing anything

Pro Not Being Sick

- I will be in control of my life

- my self-esteem will go up

- I will be able to make more choices

- I will be able to make money, get the degree, and accomplish my goals

- I can attract other healthy, competent people

- I will be moving in the direction of my dreams

- I will be able to have kids and take care of them because I know how to take care of myself

- my family will stop worrying about me

- my doctors won't be bothering me so much

Con Not Being Sick

- no one will take care of me

- no one will feel sorry for me

- I will have to be responsible

- I will have to work hard to accomplish goals

- I won't have any excuses anymore

Try making your own pro and con list, and decide for yourself. It helped me to identify the reasons why I was not getting well, so that I could soul search and begin to allow wellness into my life. It helped me make the

choice, and it can help you, too.

Inspirational Writing

"One in Five"*
by: Emily Grossman, MA

One in five, one in five

Maybe Jenna down in Marketing,
Max, who bartends at the dive,
Even Nate, the hairdresser,
Who really hates to drive
Could be the one in five

Maybe Diane from class,
Theo, who juggles knives,
Or Anna from Workout World
Who eats protein bars
To stay alive
Could be the one in five

Is it Patrice the au pair,
Or Janika in sales?
Or Cousin Alex in Nevada
Who collects all those snails?

Rather than hypothesize,
Let's all try to empathize,
Use reason and don't stigmatize-
By now you should realize
That *ANYONE*
Could be the one in five.

* One in five Americans adults suffer from a diagnosable mental disorder in a given year
according to The National Institute of Mental Health:
http://www.nimh.nih.gov/publicat/numbers.cfm

Spotlight on Recovery: Carol Kivler

Carol's energy is contagious. Just spend a day with her and you become caught up in the whirlwind of charisma and enthusiasm that define her effervescent personality. Carol wears many hats. In her public life, she is a speaker, author, coach, and corporate trainer. In her private life, she is a mother and grandmother. She is also a survivor of a major and recurrent mental illness, or a consumer.

In Carol's presence, it is easy to forget that she has had bouts with depression so severe that she had to receive electroconvulsive therapy (ECT). She has a very "up" personality, and is always speaking about new and creative ideas for her two businesses. Her first business, Kivler Communications (www.kivlercommunications.com), has been successful for many years, but is growing larger all the time. In this business, Carol does speaking, coaching, and training with a self-help emphasis. Her clients include anyone from large corporations such as Ernst and Young to major universities such as Princeton.

Carol has also authored and coauthored two books. The first, *Fantastic Customer Service Inside and Out*, is a book in which customer service people from around the country give their advice. Her chapter is entitled "What It Takes to Give 'And Then Some' Service." The other book is an interactive journal entitled *Blessings: My Journal of Gratitude.*

After working in the speaking business for sometime, this entrepreneur had another brilliant idea for a business. She decided to use her experiences with mental illness to start Courageous Recovery (www.courageousrecovery.com), another business in which she speaks about her experiences with depression. Carol speaks to associations, organizations, corporations, school systems, and government agencies in order to "raise awareness to remove the stigma of mental illness and to instill hope in those who live with it."[1] Carol has had much success with this. Her clients have given her rave reviews. One nursing student from Seton Hall University writes: "Bravo! Carol! Your personal story was extremely enlightening both personally and professionally. Not only did you take the negative stigma away from mental illness for me, you reinforced the very reason why I chose to go into nursing in the first place - to make a difference."[2] Carol is really doing her part to eradicate stigma.

---

[1] www.courageousrecovery.com
[2] ibid

When asked why she does such work, Carol says that she believes that God gave her this illness for a reason. She believes that it is her job to speak out and help others who are struggling as well as to make people aware that mental illness is nothing to be ashamed of. She says that she thinks that in the next couple of years, we are going to see less and less stigma, and she wants to be at the forefront of the movement to de-stigmatize the illness. Carol, it would seem that you are already there!

Spotlight on Recovery: Robin Cunningham

Robin has lived an extremely remarkable life. After receiving his MBA, Robin began a challenging business career. Within three years, he advanced to the level of Vice President and thereafter, he served as a senior corporate officer with several international industry-leading corporations, or their subsidiaries, as well as a major Wall Street investment banking firm and a highly profitable commercial bank. He was involved in corporate turnarounds, acquisitions, and divestitures, and was instrumental in the formation of four new ventures. He has served as a Managing Director, Director, Chief Executive Officer, Chief Operating Officer, Executive Vice President, as well as the

Chief Corporate Officer in Finance, Sales, Marketing, Administration and Strategic Planning.

Robin's accomplishments are unusual given that from the age of thirteen, he has suffered from schizophrenia, perhaps the most devastating of all mental illnesses. Schizophrenia is a condition that is genetically linked, and is characterized by abnormal brain chemistry and aberrant thinking processes. Robin has experienced the ravages of paranoia, delusions of grandeur, hallucinations, thought insertions, distorted thinking, altered perceptions, anxiety, depression and delusion-based operant behaviors. He has been hospitalized twice.

In 1956, when Robin's illness first appeared, the prognosis for individuals suffering from schizophrenia was dismal. For years, he dealt with the mental and emotional agonies characteristic of his condition. Leading a double life, partly in the real world and partly in a surreal world, he struggled with the debilitating effects of his illness. But with the aid of Dr. Sol Levy, an extraordinary psychiatrist 30 years ahead of his peers, he began a long search for an efficacious medication and learned highly effective coping skills. After ten years and many trials, a medication was found that completely restored Robin's functionality. The many coping mechanisms he had learned then became personal growth guidelines, or "tools," that have contributed greatly to his success. Still, Robin must deal with his schizophrenia on a day-to-day basis, and remains dependent upon his medication.

Robin's life experience has provided him with intriguing insights into the human condition. Since his retirement, he has devoted himself to writing, public speaking and to advocacy for the mentally ill. He currently

serves on the New Jersey Governor's Council on Mental
Health Stigma. He has written a body of poetry, and is
presently writing a memoir relating his experiences with
schizophrenia.

Copyright Robin Cunningham 2001

"Dandelions"

I remember as a child, I used to love to go and pick dandelions. I would make bouquets and crowns for my hair. I loved their yellow color; they were bright like the sun. I would wear my crown and pretend that I was a sun goddess. I loved it when they turned light and wispy so that I could make a wish and blow the white fuzzy top off the flower. I truly believed that this would make all of my dreams come true instantly.

One day, my father called me inside.

"Emily," he said sternly, "after today, you will not be able to go out and play with the dandelions anymore.

Dandelions are weeds and we must get rid of them. I am having men come tomorrow to kill all of the dandelions," he said.

I cried and cried, but I couldn't get him to change his mind. I just couldn't understand. How could such beautiful flowers be considered weeds? If there were roses growing in the grass, my father wouldn't have killed them. But, once you called a dandelion a weed, it had to be dealt with in a different way. I became angry. What I didn't realize at the time was that I was angry because people stigmatize dandelions by calling them weeds; I saw them for what they were - beautiful flowers.

Just like those dandelions, we stigmatize those with mental illness. Just like all people, people with mental illness have many gifts and the potential to do wonderful things with their lives. Yet, in many cases, we impose limits on them, assuming that they cannot have the same life as "normal" people. We call them names, we keep them from getting jobs because we think they can't handle them, we even sometimes feel it would be better if they were locked away somewhere so that we wouldn't have to deal with them. Just like the dandelions, our impulse is to remove them from our presence, rather than see that they too are beautiful flowers with the potential to "bloom" and do wonderful things in this world.

I dream of a society where we do not stigmatize anymore. I dream of a society where dandelions are not weeds, but are flowers that can grow freely. I dream of a place where people with mental illnesses are not called "crazy" or labeled in any other way, but are free to live up to their full potential without being constantly stigmatized for an illness that they did not cause, but was given to them through heredity. This is my wish. Now where's a dandelion when you need one, anyway?

Resources and Putting it All Together

So, I hope that this book has given you a bit of a start in understanding mood disorders, and how to recover. I want to repeat for the last time that it is going to take patience and time to get better. BE KIND to yourself.

In the meantime, as you are recovering, I am going to give you some other helpful resources that you can reach out to that may aid in the process.

1. National Alliance on Mental Illness

http://www.nami.org/

This is a wonderful organization that runs support groups for consumers and families. It also is extremely active in advocacy.

2. Mental Health Association of NJ

http://www.mhanj.org/

Offers support services for those who are struggling with mental illness, including professional development.

3. Division of Vocational Rehabilitation of NJ

http://lwd.dol.state.nj.us/labor/dvrs/DVRIndex.html

This organization helps consumers to get back into the workforce.

4. Dialectical Behavioral Therapy Website

www.dbtselfhelp.com

This is a wonderfully helpful website which teaches all about the DBT Therapy that I mentioned earlier.

5. The Dream Team Coaches

www.emilygrossmansdreamteam.net

This is the site for my personal business, in which I coach children and young adults with mind disorders. I also maintain a blog about mental health on this site.

Good Luck, and Be Well!

Love,

Emily ☺

Made in the USA
Lexington, KY
28 January 2013